MOMStories

Quiet Contemplations for Mothers

Vickie LoPiccolo Jennett

with contemplation questions

by Paula Hagen, OSB

Resource Publications, Inc.
San Jose, California

This book is dedicated to all grandmothers,
especially mine:

Genevieve Cecelia Sipe
and
Filomena Mano LoPiccolo

Reprint Department
Resource Publications, Inc.
160 E. Virginia Street #290
San Jose, CA 95112-5876
(408) 286-8505 voice
(408) 287-8748 fax

Library of Congress Cataloging-in-Publication Data
Jennett, Vickie LoPiccolo, 1955–
    MOMStories: quiet contemplations for mothers / Vickie LoPiccolo Jennett; with contemplation questions by Paula Hagen.
        p.   cm.
    Includes indexes.
    ISBN 0-89390-505-4 (pbk.)
        1. Mothers—Prayer-books and devotions—English. 2. Motherhood
    —Religious aspects—Christianity—Meditations. I. Title: MOMstories.
II. Hagen, Paula, 1937– III. Title.
    BV4847 .J455 2000
    242'.6431—dc21   99-045839

Printed in the United States of America
00 01 02 03 04 | 5 4 3 2 1

Editor: Nick Wagner
Production coordinator: Mike Sagara
Copyeditor: Laura Quilling
Cover design: Mike Sagara and Ken Guentert

Contents

Before you move on ...

At no time in history have the human nerves suffered as they do now from the wild speed at which life travels, and the pressures of occupations and amusements.

When do you think this quotation was penned? Last month? Last year? A decade ago? Try more than a century ago!

Funny how the very advances that make life more convenient and save us time and energy are often the very same things that complicate our lives. Would the author of those words be more harried or more relaxed in our twenty-first-century world? The answer to that question eludes me.

Well, if only for a few moments, put away both mental and physical clutter and take time for these *Quiet Contemplations for Mothers*. Just trying to get this manuscript out the door in time convinced me that I'll take peace and serenity any way I can get it. If I can't be outside listening to the birds' songs each morning when the sun comes up, five minutes of peace in the shower will have to do. If I can't seem to budget an elusive week in Hawaii each year (I managed it twice in my life), a weekend in the mountains will be just fine. If I just can't squeeze in a semester-long spirituality class, a few minutes with a book by a wise and learned philosopher just might suffice. We need to savor peace wherever we can find it.

Truth be known, there are days when I head upstairs intent on retrieving a book or magazine or some other item from my bedside table. When I get to the top of the stairs, I'm distracted by an errant pair of dirty socks. The offending socks compel me to gather up a complete load of darks, grab some Excedrin for the backache that came from falling asleep on the couch the night before, and head down to the washing machine. Suddenly, I ask myself why I actually went upstairs in the first place.

Do I have a problem? Nothing major. I'm just suffering from an epidemic that plagues many mothers today. That epidemic is overload.

We want to do the best possible job of caring for our families—their spiritual, emotional, and physical well-being are of paramount importance to us. We strive to excel at our work—whether it's creating ceramics at the studio, packing sack lunches for the kids, or crunching figures for the corporation's annual report. We feel obligated to help with the historic preservation campaign (who wants a four-lane road barreling through downtown landmarks?). "No" isn't in our vocabulary when teachers need assistance in the copy room. More midnight cries bring us weary-eyed into our toddlers' bedrooms. Our grandsons' school plays conflict with our bowling nights. Our college kids need help finding medicine to get through bouts with stomach flu (halfway across the country). Our husbands have this great camping adventure planned; could "we" do the packing? And who's going to take care of that leaky toilet?

Well, I actually think a leaky toilet is where *Quiet Contemplations for Mothers* had its origin. I was lying in bed one evening, attempting to come up with a clever way to tie together this third collection of stories by and for mothers. The sheets were Downy fresh; the breeze outside was relaxing. Some nondescript yet soothing tune was wafting from the radio. All was well with the world—except that darn toilet. It had been running for ten or fifteen minutes, as it had the night before and the night before that. So I finally got up, adjusted the float, and headed back to bed—no luck. It took three more trips before the float was properly adjusted. (Of course, my husband slumbered all the while, oblivious, next to me.)

Quiet—I just wanted peace and quiet. I wanted time to think about the day without interruption. How is it, I wondered, that our lives as mothers always seem to present us with that one last nose to wipe, one last meeting to attend, or one last bill to pay? Although many of these interruptions are in fact what bring us great pleasure, we just don't have enough time for quiet contemplation. There it was: Out of chaos and a noisy toilet came peace and quiet. Along with the silence, I found a title to tie together the stories that mothers so willingly agreed to share with one another.

Everywhere we turn, books, magazines, workshops, and seminars are suggesting ways to simplify our lives. There are scores of formulas, plans, and prescriptions (no, not the Prozac type) for how to do this. We can get rid of physical clutter and clear our calendars, but I'm beginning to believe that true simplicity and peace are even more elusive than wisdom and patience.

Yet through it all, we are holy women of God.

The picture was clarified for me one afternoon when I stopped by our parish to drop off some paperwork for one of the ministries. I needed a key to get into a downstairs office. As luck would have it, the receptionist was a substitute. Just as I was attempting to convince him that it was okay to lend the key to a stranger, our associate pastor walked up, put his arm around me, looked at the receptionist, and said, "Don't worry about her; she's a holy woman of God."

You know how sometimes simple comments strike a chord in your heart? Well, this one did. As I headed down the stairs, key in hand, and my brow furrowed, I pondered, "Who, me? Holy?"

Then I smiled. Why not? I might not be the very essence of holiness, but I do try to lead a holy life—you know, do the right thing for the right reason at the right time. Live the Gospel as best I can. Right then, I was finishing off yet another of the many volunteer projects I've done over the years for church, school, the neighborhood, and civic groups. Then I was on my way to pick up my youngest at soccer before heading over to visit my grandmother.

You bet my life is frantic and busy and far from perfect, but it's also holy. I realized then, if just for a moment, how blessed my life is—blessed with wonderful people and relationships, with health and happiness. Life is holy, simply holy. All I could do was recognize this and smile. It is my wish that these stories from other holy mothers will help you see the simple holiness in our lives.

With Gratitude

Thanks to all the women who contributed to MOMStories. Your comments in classes, retreats, workshops, MOMS groups, and newsletters are the basis for these inspiring glimpses at God's presence in our lives. Your e-mail messages, faxes, and letters are encouraging and inspiring. Your willingness to share heartfelt emotions will enrich the lives of mothers everywhere. Thanks especially to these women for their wit, wisdom, support, and stories:

Maryann Avery	Connie A. Grismer	Judy Matthews
Kate Bernat	Jo Anne Gburek	Lisa Mulato
Jan Petroni Brown	Paula Gonzalez	Emily Novak
Krystal K. Brown	Happenings in	Paula Patterson
Monica Charnell	the Heartland	Katie Rains
Adria D. Clark	Lori Hately	Margo Reeves
Betty Clewell	Roberta Hazelbaker	Kristin Sartor
Pat Miller Cook	Maggie Herrod	Becky Schaller
Denise Drew	Lisa Johannes	Sheri Stevenson
Laura Dodson	Michele W. Korth	Karen Thomason
Jane Ferraro	Mary Kraus	Eileen Thompson
Lisa Frazier	Terese Lamontagne	Joan V. Throm
Susan Gienane	Jean Lea	Martha VanZant
JoAnne Gburek	Mayra Lingvay	Bonnie Voirin
Susan Glenane	Mary Ann Locklear	Cindy Westhoff

Acknowledgments

The Scripture quotations contained herein, unless marked otherwise, are from the New Revised Standard Version of the Bible, Catholic Edition, copyrighted 1993, by the Division of Christian Education of the National Council of the Churches of Christ in the United States of America, and are used by permission. All rights reserved.

Scripture texts marked "NAB" are taken from the *New American Bible with Revised New Testament* Copyright © 1986 by the Confraternity of Christian Doctrine, 3211 4th Street, N.E., Washington, D.C. 20017-1194 and are used by permission of the copyright owner. All Rights Reserved.

The "Rules for Ongoing Groups," page 67, is reprinted from MOMS: *Developing a Ministry* by Paula Hagen and Patricia Hoyt, © 1995 Resource Publications Inc., and is used with permission. All rights reserved.

Quotation on page vi taken from *The History of Underclothes* by C. Willet & Phillis Cunnington (New York: Dover, 1992), p. 184. Originally published in 1951.

More MOMStories?

You are invited to continue telling and sending your MOMStories to wordsbyvic@prodigy.net or faxing them to (480) 895-2214.

2

*Make me to know your ways, O LORD; / teach me your paths.
Lead me in your truth, and teach me, / for you are the God of my
salvation; / for you I wait all day long. / Psalm 25:4–5*

Compassion

Lord, becoming a mother brought so many changes to my life.
Sure, there were the physical changes—I lost my girlish figure,
had bags under my eyes, and never got enough sleep. But more
important were the spiritual changes. My sense of compassion
deepened. I had a new perspective on your precious gift of life.

One night at a church function, I learned that a friend had
cancer. Prayer, medical attention, and support would be her
salvation. I choked back the tears, wondering how long I would
have to savor this gift of motherhood. When I arrived home that
night, I went into my son's room, lifted him out of his crib, and
held him as tears trickled down my face.

Then I remember watching the Oklahoma City bombing
coverage on TV and weeping as I held this baby in my arms.
How many people in Oklahoma City would never see their
children again? I also remember awakening to headlines about the
Littleton disaster. Again, I wept, this time at the kitchen table.

Before having children, these news stories would have been
just stories worthy of news coverage. Now they affect my very
being, my inner core, my soul. Even on the roughest days (and
there are quite a few of them when toddlers are involved), the
compassion that has been awakened in me stirs in my head
another chorus of a favorite song: "God is in control. We believe
that his children will not be forsaken …"

For Contemplation
• How have I learned to relish the special graces of motherhood?
• In what ways has my compassion been heightened since
  becoming a mother?
• How can Advent be a time for me to journey along the path of
  truth and hope?

[I am] constantly praying with joy in every one of my prayers for all of you. … / Philippians 1:4

God's gift to me

One December morning, I woke up with excruciating pain pulsing through my left arm. I figured I had just hurt my arm while lugging children and suitcases through airports en route to visit my parents for Christmas. The holidays came and went, and the pain intensified. For five months, I was shifted from doctor to physical therapist to doctor. Chronic pain is depressing and debilitating. For the first time, I could relate to friends who had lived for years under the cloud of pain. It is so easy to want to stay in bed day after day and so difficult to be optimistic when even the simplest of tasks can't be performed.

Finally in May, an MRI isolated my problem—a herniated disk. Meanwhile, I had come to realize that although I was suffering, there were others living in even more spiritual and emotional pain. Rather than praying selfish prayers for the elimination of my pain, I connected with God to pray for others. After all, God knows me—always has and always will.

Then, in July, I learned that my condition was very serious, and I needed immediate surgery. Following surgery, while I lived for two months on my couch, staring straight ahead because of the restrictive hard plastic collar, God poured his love, peace, grace, and beauty into my life through prayers, flowers, phone calls, people, and meals. As I pondered how I could possibly repay every kindness, it dawned on me that I did not have to. My job just then was to receive, to allow my friends to "wash my feet." Basking in God's grace and goodness was enlightening.

For Contemplation
- When do I feel God's presence in others?
- How can I remember to pray more quiet and humble thank yous?
- How is openness to God's graces part of my Advent journey?

4

Have no anxiety at all, but in everything, by prayer and petition, with thanksgiving, make your requests known to God. / Philippians 4:4–7

Waiting and thinking

I was in a doctor's waiting room one morning when a television promo asked, "Remember when television used to be fun?"

Under her breath, a woman next to me sighed, "Remember when *life* used to be fun?"

I smiled, made light of the comment, and said, "Yup, things can get pretty hectic sometimes."

Then I sat there wondering why our lives aren't more fun. Since the wait was longer than usual, my mind had plenty of time to ponder. I came to the conclusion that worry and anxiety are what frequently get in the way of fun. Oh sure, we need to concern ourselves with basic health and safety, but other than that, why do we spend so much energy on worry?

As mothers, we seem to worry from the time our children are born. Will they walk on time? Talk clearly? Will they have good friends? Good teachers? Will they work to the best of their abilities or get sidetracked? Will they respect others? Heck, will they love and respect themselves? Will they make the right choices? Will they avoid trouble? Will they know true happiness? Will they grow up anxious?

Concern is one thing, constant worry is another. There are some things we truly can control, but others that we have to turn over to God. By prayer and petition, we make our needs known to God, who loves our children infinitely more than we can. Then we can free our hearts to enjoy the life God gave us.

For Contemplation
- What steps can I take to reduce the unhealthy stress and undo unnecessary anxiety in my life?
- How can I allow Advent's holy message of hope to inspire my everyday activities?
- When worry consumes me, how can I learn to turn to God, to friends, or to family in my Christian community?

"And blessed is she who believed that there would be a fulfillment of what was spoken to her by the Lord." / Luke 1:45

Messages from angels

I was very anxious to become pregnant and have our long-desired child. After a miscarriage, it was the first time we could try to conceive again. One night I woke up out of a deep sleep—sleeping on my left side, snuggled up to my husband—and there at the foot of our bed stood a beautiful angel, my Guardian Angel. I knew it was her: I recognized her wings and long blond hair. As I felt her hands on me, I understood her unspoken message that we would have a healthy baby. Sure enough, a week and a half later, my home pregnancy test told us I was pregnant.

The first trimester was especially frightening because of the previous miscarriage. But, throughout the pregnancy, I had my angel's message as security. I think this was the first time I truly believed in the power of faith. Coincidentally, our daughter was born three weeks early—on my birthday.

Then two years later, we again tried to conceive a child. One night, when I was rocking our daughter, I noticed a light flickering on the Christmas tree. It was the one that lit the manger scene. I moved the ornament to another light, and that light started flickering the same way. I looked through the tree to the wall, and there was the image of my angel, the same one who visited my bed a few years prior. I knew then that I was pregnant.

For Contemplation
- Do I believe that God attempts to get my attention in daily events?
- Christ's love lights the world, not only at Christmas but all year long. What can I do to help keep this light burning in my own home and in my heart?
- In what ways can I take better care of my spiritual needs and the spiritual needs of those I love?

But Mary treasured all these words and pondered them in her heart.
   Luke 2:19

Hearts come home to Jesus at Christmas

Because of my job in our church, I have worked every Christmas
Eve for the past fourteen years. When I had an opportunity to
share Christmas with my daughter's family last year, it was with
great joy and some trepidation. I was anxious to visit their new
home and parish, yet somewhat hesitant because I would be away
from my own faith community.

   Because my daughter was music director for her parish's
Christmas Eve family mass, I knew the experience would be a
treat. Not only that, but she also told me I would meet a
wonderful priest who had long ago been given permission to adopt
ten children, now grown with children of their own.

   During the homily, he shared a story about one of his
grandchildren. It seems the parent received a note from the child's
teacher saying the child was spoiled. The grandfather called the
teacher and confirmed that, indeed, the child was spoiled because
she was a child of God. He went on to say that we all are spoiled
because of the great love God has for us and shared with us
through the birth of his Son. I was reminded of that great love as
the liturgy continued. At the communion meditation, my
daughter prayerfully sang, "Mary, Did You Know." Hearing her
beautiful voice was wonderful, but nothing could compare with
the joy of having my own spoiled five-year-old granddaughter
cuddling in my lap and singing with her mother so softly that no
one else could hear. Through my tears, I realized that these gifts
of tradition and faith were the best I could ever receive.

For Contemplation
+ What can I do to share the treasures of our faith tradition?
+ When do I cry tears of joy? Tears that express gratitude?
+ How can I realize more fully what it means to be a child of God?

As God's chosen ones, holy and beloved, clothe yourselves with compassion, kindness, humility, meekness, and patience. Bear with one another and, if anyone has a complaint against another, forgive each other. … / Colossians 3:12–13

Holy family treasures

My son has a stuffed dog named "Barkus." My mom and dad gave it to him when he was only one. Needless to say, Barkus is a very special pal. My son takes him everywhere—to bed, in the car, to Grandma's, shopping. While getting ready for kindergarten one day, my son walked into the bathroom to find his year-old sister putting Barkus in the toilet. At that moment, I thought that five years of trying to instill the virtues of gentleness, kindness, forgiveness, and love in my son was about to go down the toilet too. But just as my son let out a big howl, I realized everything was going to be okay.

"Ohhh," he said falling down on his knees. "It's all right. I forgive you because you're my baby sister, and you don't know any better. I still love you."

Then he hugged her.

I was overjoyed with the knowledge that I might have laid a foundation for my son who just might be growing toward the strong, gentle, loving man that I pray he will someday be.

For Contemplation
• When are the times that I recognize the fruits of my labors as a mother? How can I celebrate these moments?
• What rituals do we have that celebrate ordinary affection and holiness in our homes?
• How do we practice forgiveness of one another in our families?

My Thoughts

The LORD bless you and keep you; / the LORD make his face to shine upon you, and be gracious to you; / the LORD lift up his countenance upon you, and give you peace. / Numbers 6:24–26

God's love transcends all

Six months into my pregnancy, we discovered that my baby's heart had stopped beating. My fears were confirmed by ultrasound. Although my baby was gone, I continued on with the worry mothers know so well. Most of those worries centered around why he died, but one fear stood out among the rest. How would my son know where to go when he got to heaven? Would there be anyone to show him the way? The thought of a lost child not knowing where to go was painful. I would not be the one to guide him home.

Then, on the morning of his birth, I experienced God's healing grace. I prayed, placing my concerns before God. As I dozed, I felt a comforting presence. When I opened my eyes, no one except my husband was there. As the night progressed, I sensed that others had joined us in the room. Although I couldn't make out the faces or even the shapes, I knew that these were family members who had gone to heaven. They kept growing in number as daylight approached. The room felt so full.

Just before my son was born, I realized that God had heard my plea. These heavenly relatives were there to take my son home. It was no coincidence that my son, Daniel, was born at sunrise. This was God's way of showing me that there is light after darkness and that peace can be found even in pain. As I held my son for the first and last time, uttering hello and good-bye in the same breath, my worries were gone. I was at peace. God's grace gave me a love that transcends time and distance, heaven and earth, life and death.

For Contemplation
• How does God speak to me when I'm confused?
• What can I learn from the faith of my friends or ancestors?
• What is the most comforting presence I have ever experienced?

Wisdom praises herself,
  and tells of her glory in the midst of her people. / Sirach 24:1

Amazing grace

A three-year-old running through the house in stocking feet on a shiny wood floor is a definite no-no in our home. That's not to say it never happens. In fact, one evening those very antics led us to the emergency room. When my daughter fell, the first words out of my mouth were the overused, "I told you, 'No running in the house!'"

That said, I hugged her and asked where she was hurt. She pointed to the back of her head, and I pulled her hair back only to discover an inch-long gash. After arranging care for the other children, we were off to the emergency room.

By the time we were seen, my daughter had calmed down. I, however, was quite anxious. In an effort to help her through the stitches, I offered to sing a song. Throughout the procedure and my humble efforts to sing, the doctors and nurses continuously commented on what a brave little girl she was. Even a young man next to us—who was there for dehydration—looked up and smiled at my daughter's peaceful demeanor. Not being comfortable singing solos in public, I know it was simply God's grace that allowed me to minister to my daughter and anyone within earshot about his "Amazing Grace."

For Contemplation
- Many time-honored songs reveal the gifts and graces of God. How can I incorporate these messages as I go about the task of ministering to my family and friends?
- Are there ways that I can be more aware of the grace God sets before me each day?
- Physical pain and suffering is a very real part of our lives. What is my response to pain and suffering?

My Thoughts

For he delivers the needy when they call,
  the poor and those who have no helper.
He has pity on the weak and the needy,
  and saves the lives of the needy. / Psalm 72:12–13

The right place at the right time

For years, my husband and I had tried to conceive a child. By this point, I was on medication that made me sick. We wanted so much to become parents. We started talking about adoption.

Then one Sunday in our church bulletin, we noticed an announcement for an adoption meeting. We took that as God's sign that we were on the right path. We went to the meeting, talked about our decision, and started the paperwork.

The long and complicated process of becoming certified for adoption requires that the adoptive parents undergo medical checkups. The doctor who examined me mentioned that he had been adopted through Catholic Social Services. God was giving us yet another sign.

Being at the right place at the right time felt so comfortable.

Once we were certified, it was only eleven months until we received a child, our blessing from God.

For Contemplation
• How can I be more aware of the many messages and messengers that God sends my way?
• Poverty takes many forms and certainly not all of them have to do with material well-being. What are some of the afflictions in my life, and how can I accept them with God's help?
• What do I do when it seems God isn't listening to my pleas?

My Thoughts

"I truly understand that God shows no partiality ...." / Acts 10:34

The grace of forgiveness

My daughter was eighteen years old when I moved from New York to North Carolina to get married. Both of us had been in counseling, and I was confident that she would be okay. This, coupled with my counselor's suggestion that I needed to get on with my life, gave me the reassurance to move on even though my daughter chose to remain in her birth city.

Several years later, my daughter told me she wasn't okay and felt abandoned. She was still angry about my leaving her. I felt bad about this but didn't know how to make it right for both of us. I decided to write a birthday letter asking her forgiveness. I didn't offer excuses, but I did tell her that I had trusted our counselor and didn't realize the impact the move would have on her.

Her only reply was, "Someday, Mom, I'll get past my anger, and I'll write to you with the response you are seeking."

About six months later, I went on a retreat. At one point, we were directed to a chapel and given several letters from people who were praying for us. My daughter's was the last one I opened. The words, "I forgive you, Mom, for everything," will live in my heart as a precious treasure for the rest of my life.

The next time I spoke with my daughter, I explained that she had given me the greatest possible gift. Although we still live apart, we are closer than we have ever been.

For Contemplation
- What special moments of grace have I recently experienced?
- How would I describe my relationship with someone who abandoned me?
- What are some ways that I can become a more forgiving person?

My Thoughts

Now concerning spiritual gifts ... there are a variety of gifts, but the same Spirit; and there are varieties of services, but the same Lord; and there are varieties of activities, but it is the same God who activates all of them in everyone. / 1 Corinthians 12:4–6

She ministered to all of us

How can I describe a special woman who changed my life and the lives of all who met her?

She was an extraordinary woman. Although wheelchair-bound, this gifted woman participated and shared in so many ways. She ministered to her friends, showing each of us how to love God, even through life's deepest trials. She cared so genuinely about everyone she met. She saw so much good in everything and in everyone.

We lost her several years ago due to complications of muscular dystrophy. Our hearts were broken, but her gifts of love, compassion, and humility sustained us. Even today her light shines in each one of us as we remember her spirit.

I thank God for the gift of this woman in my life. She truly was a spiritual gift.

For Contemplation
- Each of us encounters amazingly special people who bring priceless gifts into our lives. Who has been that person (or persons) in my life? What was their gift?
- What can I do to inspire friends who need to be lifted from the depths of despair?
- How is God trying to show me the many spiritual gifts in my life?

My Thoughts

The law of the LORD is perfect,
  reviving the soul;
the decrees of the LORD are sure,
  making wise the simple;
the precepts of the LORD are right,
  rejoicing the heart;
the commandment of the LORD is clear,
  enlightening the eyes …. / Psalm 19:7–8

Writing letters to God

I know God hears my prayers, but sometimes it helps me to write them down. As I reread them, I see and hear God's wisdom and see God's grace working in my life.

Dear God,
For so many years, I was lost without you. I was so selfish. I didn't need anyone but myself. I went through many one-sided relationships in which I was looking to be loved. Now I know I didn't need the love or approval of others. I needed to open my heart and give my useless anxieties to you, for you are my loving God. Thank you for helping me find the inner wisdom that was there all along.
Love,
One of your children

This is just one of many letters I've written God, whom I've grown to know, trust, and love.

For Contemplation
- When did I first realize that God had given me some wisdom inside myself?
- How do I listen to that wisdom deep inside myself?
- How have I learned to love God and to allow God to refresh my soul?

Love is patient; love is kind; love is not envious or boastful or arrogant or rude. It does not insist on its own way; it is not irritable or resentful; it does not rejoice in wrongdoing, but rejoices in the truth. It bears all things, believes all things, hopes all things, endures all things. Love never ends. / 1 Corinthians 13:4–8

Love given and received

He was very seldom hugged or kissed, my little four-year-old neighbor. He was such a sweet boy, the middle child in a family with three boys. I'm not ashamed to say that he was my favorite of all the neighborhood children. I was a big hugger—truth be known, probably an annoying hugger—and kisser too. I adore kids.

Although we moved from that neighborhood, we went back to visit with our old friends a few years later. The place was crowded with everyone buzzing around. The couch was filled, but my favorite former little neighbor managed to squeeze in next to me. To my delight, I felt his small arm slowly crawl across my back and squeeze me tight. I looked down at him, and tears came to my eyes as he said, "I love you."

Sweet moments like this are among those I treasure. They are experiences that reinforce the importance of the little things and little people, the meaning of unspoken kindnesses, and the joy of giving and receiving hugs.

For Contemplation
- What can I do right now to become more conscious of the little acts of kindness and the special little people in my life?
- Do I remember to give freely of myself even when it seems my gift of self is not received?
- How do I reach out to love others on a daily basis?

My Thoughts

"Master we have worked all night but have caught nothing." / Luke 5:5

Can you lend a hand?

I always thought that being strong and self-sufficient was the only way to be. I had to be in control the whole time. "You can do it," was the message my dad always taught me.

Slowly, over time, I have finally come to realize that it's okay to let go. At long last, the saying "Let go and let God" is starting to feel comfortable to me. I no longer see letting go as a sign of weakness. I am humble enough to recognize that maybe I can't do everything all the time. I realize that asking for God's help is okay too.

In addition, I'm slowly approaching a stage in my life in which I am able to get close enough to and comfortable enough with people that I can ask them for help. Nonetheless, giving up the self-sufficiency that I've worked a lifetime to achieve still isn't easy. Yet, as my relationship with God becomes more comfortable—I see God as a sort of friend, mentor, and protector—I am more able to trust God's love in others too.

I no longer look at reaching out for help as a weakness or a failure. In fact, there is a certain strength in knowing that I truly do need to reach out and seek a helping hand.

For Contemplation
- How is letting go different than giving up?
- What relics from my growing-up years are keeping me from moving forward in personal growth or relationships? What steps can I take to promote healing?
- What has helped me to turn to God and friends for help?

My Thoughts

*Blessed are you who are poor, / for yours is the kingdom of God.
Blessed are you who are hungry now, / for you will be filled. / Blessed
are you who weep now, / for you will laugh. / Blessed are you when
people hate you, and when they exclude you, revile you, and defame
you on account of the Son of Man. / Luke 6:20–22*

A special bond

My son was born with a very rare genetic condition that is passed
from mother to sons. It requires him to take medication, carry an
emergency injection, and be cautious with activities.

When my second son was born, my two daughters and son had
an early opportunity to meet the baby and bond with him. We
already knew that he had inherited the genetic disease, so we told
the older kids. My daughters each held him, rocked him, and
talked about changing his diapers, feeding him, and babysitting.

My older son, however, had a different take on the situation.
He held his brother for a long time, looking at him and explaining
as best he could the condition they shared. "I will always be there
for you," he said. "This is something that's ours to share. I'll help
you with your medicine and carry your shot."

Finally, when he was ready to pass the bundle back to me, he
looked up and said, "He understands that it's me, him, and God
against the world."

This innocent and brave comment gave me both a chuckle and
a lump in my throat. My oldest son, who was so alone with his
condition, was no longer alone. He saw a purpose to his
condition—he was there to help his little brother. I, too, grew a
step closer to God that day knowing that even after I'm gone, the
boys would have each other and their special bond.

For Contemplation
- When have my hardships been turned into blessings?
- How does it feel to experience reaching out to others because
  I know how they feel?
- What lessons have I recently learned from my children?

Love your enemies, do good to those who hate you, bless those who curse you, pray for those who abuse you. ... Do to others as you would have them do to you." / Luke 6:27–28,31

Taking time to understand

One Sunday morning I anxiously scanned the congregation at our church looking for friends I had invited to my husband's surprise birthday party. I had mailed the invitation two weeks prior, yet I had not received a response from these close friends. I approached them in a bit of a rush and asked, "You'll be coming to the party. Right?"

Before I got the words out of my mouth, my friend's head was shaking back and forth. "Why not?" I asked abruptly.

His wife explained that they had been to the restaurant where the party was to take place, and she had to leave because of the smoky conditions.

I interrupted the answer, insisting that because the party was in a separate room, she would be fine. Defending their decision and expressing regret, our friend blamed the restaurant's air-conditioning filtering system.

Once I got home and had a chance to reflect on the situation, I realized that I had offered no compassion whatsoever toward my friend's lung condition or toward their disappointment at not being able to celebrate with their treasured friend. I was moved to call later that afternoon, offering an apology for being so insensitive. My friend assured me that I had not hurt her. We laughed and talked some more as I talked about the surprise birthday plans.

I was so thankful to have asked for her forgiveness. Sometimes we just have to humble ourselves. What a perfect opportunity for God to confirm our true friends in Christ!

For Contemplation
- What lessons about humility have I learned from my own mistakes?
- Why can first impressions and snap judgments sometimes be unchristian?
- How does prayerful reflection help me see and accept situations more graciously?

Its fruit discloses the cultivation of a tree;
   so a person's speech discloses the cultivation of his mind. / Sirach 27:6

Thank you for being you

Sometimes the best impressions we leave are ones we never intended. Over the course of a year or so, I had several business dealings with a woman I met at a conference. We shared mutual friends and corresponded now and then, but we never exchanged much more than pleasantries. One day I sent her some information that elicited an unexpected thank-you note. In it, she wrote, "I knew when we first met that there was something really special about you. When I realized that you were a family ministry volunteer, I knew then what it was. Your warm glow is not man-made but spiritual. You've been a blessing to me and, I'm sure, to lots of others. Thank you for being *you*."

Warm glow? Special? Blessing? Me? Wow! This woman made my day. With heartfelt emotion and a thirty-two-cent stamp on a card decorated with angels from a 1790 engraving, she reminded me that just being myself brought joy into others' lives. I did nothing special or extraordinary. I was just myself, going about routine business and everyday activities. Yet somehow I managed to impart a glow that allowed her to see what fuels my soul. God's love truly is at work in our lives.

For Contemplation
- Just what is the "bent of my mind?"
- If the fruit of a tree shows the care it has had, what does my body say about the care I give it?
- Who has unknowingly touched my life with the love of Christ? Have I let them know?

My Thoughts

No evil shall befall you,
no scourge come near your tent.
For he will command his angels concerning you
to guard you in all your ways. / *Psalm 91:10–11*

My fears are calmed

Several years ago, my son celebrated his seventh birthday, apparently in perfect health, full of energy, and very spunky. He occupied himself quietly each morning playing on the computer. One morning I heard him coming slowly up the steps, almost like a crawl. Being half asleep, I didn't know what was happening until he stood over me saying, "I can't stop my head from shaking, and I'm talking funny."

When I looked at his face and saw the side of his mouth drooping, I knew this wasn't a dream. That morning the pediatrician said it likely was an isolated neurological episode that happens during growth spurts. Although we went home relieved, only twelve days later, the "episode" happened again. It was time to schedule some diagnostic tests. The good news was no cancer or tumors—nothing life threatening. The EEG, however, did reveal some abnormal brain wave activity that required daily medication for two years.

My grace-filled moment came shortly after his diagnosis. I was wrapping a gift in our spare bedroom, worrying that his future might be limited or seriously impaired due to the seizures. In one silent moment, I distinctly heard my mother's voice assure me, "He'll be all right." The clarity was unbelievable. It was exactly how she calmed me when I was younger. "He'll be all right" was one of the sweetest, most empowering phrases I had heard. And I knew it was true. The worrying stopped and the gratitude began. I knew God had sent the Holy Spirit to bless me that day.

For Contemplation

• Do I listen for the voices and messengers that God sends my way?
• What phrases can I repeat to maintain a sense of calm and peace?
• How can prayer help me overcome fears and anxiety?

[St. Paul encouraged the Philippians,] "Join in imitating me, and observe those who live according to the example you have in us. For many live as enemies of the cross of Christ ...." / Philippians 3:17–18

Other mothers

We all know about "other mothers." No, not the ones who spoil their kids with candy to keep them from having temper tantrums but the mothers for whom we feel sorry. The ones we look at and say, "Thank God that's not me."

The other mothers to whom I refer are the ones whose children have disabilities, or as my husband says, are "differently abled." We perceive that she experiences one disappointment after another. We pray for her yet are thankful that we aren't a member of her "club."

Well, with the birth of my fifth daughter, I unwillingly joined that club of other mothers. My beautiful baby girl was born with Down's syndrome. My heart was shattered. I kept asking God, "Why me? Why does my child have to suffer? Why will she have to work harder than her sisters to learn simple things?"

A remarkable thing happened. The more I asked God why, the more he showed me why not. I now see great miracles in small actions. I no longer take for granted developmental milestones. I now see God's face in every person. And no one knows the fate of our children until our jobs are done here on earth.

By surrendering to Jesus at the foot of the cross, I have come to understand the answer to my question of, "Why my baby?" She has taught me and my family so much more than we had ever known about God's unconditional love. Although I would not have chosen on my own to join the other mothers club, I am so thankful that God nominated me for the club.

For Contemplation
- In matters both big and small, I have opportunities to turn lemons into lemonade. What are some examples that have strengthened my life?
- How do I respond to the "crosses" in my family relationships?
- Who helps me carry my crosses?

So, if you think you are standing, watch out that you do not fall.
    1 Corinthians 10:12

Living in Christ

Our decision to raise our children in my Catholic faith has been a blessing in many ways. Before we even had children, my husband and I discussed which religion to teach our children. Since he had not been raised in any faith, he was agreeable to selecting my faith. I knew my prayers were answered when he explained his belief that no religion was perfect and that all religions were good, but because I was raised Catholic, I should practice this faith with my family and share it with our children.

One incident that reinforced the importance of our decision came when my oldest began to fear death. She wasn't comforted by my statements that death was a fact of life. My husband couldn't even talk about the subject. Then my daughter asked me whether we ever come back to life. I told her, "Yes, we do. We come back to life with Jesus and will all live again with him in God's house. We all started in heaven together and will be together again after we die."

Her face lit up like a candle, and she was never afraid of death again. Her fears were replaced with the knowledge that although we will leave this life, we will live again in heaven. I realized I had passed my faith on to my child!

For Contemplation
- How does my family handle discussions about death?
- Am I able to openly share my faith with my children? With my friends?
- How do I remember to call on the Holy Spirit to help me deal with difficult issues?

My Thoughts

So if anyone is in Christ, there is a new creation: everything old has passed away; see, everything has become new! / 2 Corinthians 5:17

A new role

I never planned to be a stepmother. Fairy tales tell us stepmothers are wicked. My tale tells quite a different story.

A decade ago I married into a package deal that included an amazing four-year-old stepdaughter. At first I resented her delaying tactics at bedtime. Soon I came to see these as holy times, times of grace, times of prayer. We set aside our independence in exchange for hugs and story time. I inscribed very special books for her—books that my grandmother inscribed to my mother, who inscribed them to me.

In the beginning I exhausted myself wanting everything to be perfect for my stepdaughter, wanting to pour myself out for her during each minute of our time together. Before long, I came to realize that she was the one pouring her richness out on me. She keeps us in laughter. She astounds us with her strength.

Fortunately for me, her definition of stepmother is friend—forget the wicked fairy-tale stuff. I thank God daily for this wonderful child, for her father, and for stories that have happy endings.

For Contemplation
- What are my parenting experiences? How do I see God's plan unfolding in them?
- When could I reach out to others to provide support for the motherhood challenges they face?
- What blessings have I received as a parent?

My Thoughts

"Let anyone among you who is without sin be the first to throw a stone at her." / John 8:7

Pregnant, again?

Whether spoken or not, I know that both friends and strangers wondered why a mother with grown children was pregnant—again. As I stumbled through typical teen trials with my oldest children, there was a child growing in my womb. I had no idea what a blessing my pregnancy would be.

First, Lord, I have to thank you for each of my children—all of the beautiful, talented people you have placed in my life and in my heart. My life has been hectic—teenagers and a full-time career left little time for me. When I first found out I was pregnant at middle age, I admit I was scared. My friends offered little support. They told me how hard my life would be, what an imposition this child would be, how my older children would resent the experience of having an infant sibling.

Then you sent me new friends—real friends, who brought joy to my pregnancy. Friends who understood my feelings. This change in my life brought me closer to you. You have consistently placed choices and signs before me. My son's sweet smile and little hands help me make good choices. He has been nothing short of a blessing. My marriage is stronger than ever. My children have discovered many things through their little brother. I now have true friends and have even been challenged to slow down, to redirect my life, to seek new possibilities. I have been challenged to look closer within my heart and move toward you.

For Contemplation
- What unexpected events have brought about changes in my life?
- How do I define true friends?
- What words would I use to describe my relationship with God?

My Thoughts

When the centurion saw what had taken place, he praised God and said, "Certainly this man was innocent." / Luke 23:47

Shared traditions

Have you ever prayed to St. Anthony for help in finding a lost item? As the patron saint of lost causes, he no doubt hears a lot of pleas day in and day out. Well, while this might be a common practice among Catholics, it's not so familiar to folks of other faiths.

Although I was raised from birth as a Roman Catholic, and although I raised my son the same way, his wife raised their children Baptist. She never objected to having them visit my church or having them discuss religion with me. Of course, the topic of St. Anthony came up from time to time, and we regularly prayed, "Dear St. Anthony, please come around. Something's lost, it must be found."

One day my six-year-old grandson called to let me know he had lost the two dollars he was supposed to take to school. Of course, he had searched everywhere for it. When I asked if he had asked St. Anthony for help, he said no, so we prayed together. I ended the phone call with a request that my grandson call me when he found it.

When he called back to tell me where he had found the two dollars, I asked if he had thanked St. Anthony for the help. "No," my grandson said, "he didn't find it, I did."

For Contemplation
- What are some new rituals I could learn?
- How does the reenactment of Christ's passion contribute to my understanding of his great sacrifice?
- God does provide for our every need. Knowing this, am I able to handle whatever life brings my way?

My Thoughts

*Therefore, let us celebrate the festival, not with the old yeast, the yeast
of malice and evil, but with the unleavened bread of sincerity and truth.*
1 Corinthians 5:8

A new vision

Four months ago I went on a retreat because I needed a safe place
to grieve. I had just returned home from caring for my
twenty-three-year-old son, who had been accidentally blinded in
his right eye by his best friend.

The weather that weekend was bleak. It matched my weary
heart, a heart that felt broken.

Today I am back at the same retreat center, but things are
different. The day is warm and comforting. I have the opportunity
to lie back on a grassy knoll by the river, feeling the sun and
breeze caress me. I even notice how the clouds seem to create a
brilliant contrast in the blue sky.

Four months ago I could only pray, "Father, let healing take
place on every level for everyone involved in this."

Today I reflected on the healing that has taken place. My son
is developing an inner vision that is profound.

For Contemplation
- When has new hope risen from tragedy or despair in my life?
- Change is difficult; fear can be a debilitating emotion. Yet, the
  power of faith and prayer can do wonders to bring new life from
  the depths of despair. How have faith and prayer worked in my
  life and the lives of those I love to create new life?
- How do I celebrate spring and new beginnings?

My Thoughts

I, John, your brother who share with you in Jesus the persecution and the kingdom and the patient endurance, was on the island called Patmos because of the word of God and the testimony of Jesus.
Revelation 1:9

Reminder of Christ's love

Thanks to my grandmother, the crucifix is a prevalent symbol in my home. Her legacy is one of love—love of the Lord and love for her family.

While growing up, I saw my grandmother a lot. She lived about an hour away, and we would celebrate every holiday with her. Sometimes she even baby-sat us. Her faith was an inspiration. In addition to going to church every day, she hung crucifixes throughout her home as a reminder of her faith.

When I was older, I knew that if I needed help with something, I could tell my grandmother. We knew she had an open line to God and believed she knew him personally. We were comforted by the fact that she would pray for us, and we cherish those memories.

Today I realize that we all have an open line to God, and I thank my grandmother for helping me understand what a great feeling it is.

For Contemplation
• When it comes to expressions of faith, the phrase "Different strokes for different folks" has some application. How do I express my faith? Are religious symbols part of this expression? Why or why not?
• When I proclaim my faith in front of others, do I ever feel threatened or ridiculed?
• How can I become more faith-filled?

My Thoughts

You have turned my mourning into dancing; / you have taken off my sackcloth / and clothed me with joy …. / O LORD my God, I will give thanks to you forever. / Psalm 30:11–12

In the midst of panic

One beautiful summer afternoon, I arrived home from picking up my ten-year-old at soccer camp to a message: The police had called to inform us that our fifteen-year-old daughter had been in a car accident. I frantically called my physician husband at work. He had just gotten a call from a colleague, who told him to head to the hospital.

En route to meet him there, I passed two semitrailers crashed along the highway. Fortunately, I had no way of knowing that the car my daughter had been riding in was smashed between them. When I arrived at the hospital, we learned that our daughter had severe head trauma. There was no way of knowing if paralysis would result. When I saw her, I couldn't believe she was hurt—she looked like an angel, not one scratch on her beautiful face. If only she would scream like her friend, who was suffering behind the next curtain with a shoulder injury.

At that moment, I was overwhelmed by fear. My head was spinning. I couldn't think. Thank God my husband took over and held our daughter's hand. I was praying, "Please God, let her be okay," when I heard a voice ask, "Where am I? What's my birthday? What did I have for dinner?" At first I was thrilled by her questions, but I was shocked a few seconds later when she asked the same three questions. She asked again and again for the next twenty-four hours. I wondered what would become of her.

She survived and so did we. Along with new gray hairs, God gave me the strength to handle the situation, whatever the outcome would be.

For Contemplation
- Sometimes when we least expect it, we find the God-given strength to go on. When is the last time that happened to me?
- What situations do I need help handling?
- How do I feel when I help others through trials and trauma?

[Jesus said,] "My sheep hear my voice. I know them, and they follow me. I give them eternal life, and they will never perish. No one will snatch them out of my hand." / John 10:27–28

A wise shepherd

She was a teacher, an especially insightful teacher, who knew and loved her students as shepherds know and love their flocks. Of course, when we were members of that flock, it drove us crazy. We thought this amazing woman had superhuman talents because she seemed to be on top of everything. What we saw as nagging truly was dedication.

She was wise but not preachy and so much more tolerant than most of our teachers. It wasn't until I reached her age that I came to realize how much energy she must have had to maintain that sparkle in her eyes. Those eyes smiled even when she was tired. I don't think this teacher ever raised her voice, even when angry students or irate parents barraged her classroom. She did her best to impart knowledge that was hard to understand and only remotely useful in the real world. How she managed to maintain our attention and interest remains a wonder to me today.

I never had a chance to tell this teacher how much she meant to me. As a student, it just didn't seem hip to let her know. When I tried to search for her after a reunion, I had no luck. It is only now as I am getting to know my own children's teachers that I realize what a treasure this humble shepherd was to her entire flock.

For Contemplation
- In what ways do I shepherd my family?
- As a member of God's flock, what can I do for the good of my brothers and sisters in Christ?
- How can I have a positive influence on the educational system?

My Thoughts

"See, the home of God is among mortals. / He will dwell with them as their God; they will be his peoples, / and God himself will be with them; he will wipe every tear from their eyes." / Revelation 21:3–4

Sunny disposition, Mom!

With those three words, my youngest is forever reminding me how important it is to stay cheerful. Does that mean I'm always happy? Heck, no. But his persistent reminders do keep me in check when I get exasperated with traffic or tired of laundry or angry at poor service. High blood pressure is about all I get from blowing my cool. He was only a preschooler when he started this ritual of imparting youthful wisdom.

Sunshine has always been an inspiration to me. As a little girl, I remember lying in bed on lazy summer mornings, watching the early light behind the curtain change from a hazy purple to peach to yellow. It amazed me that God brought us light day after day, year after year. It was something I could count on. It just happened, and to me, this was proof enough that God really did care about us.

Then in college, the experience of long, cold Midwest winters made me especially grateful for sunshine. I yearned for those early morning rays, but most days I was out the door and in the classroom before they peeked from behind the clouds. A Beatles song is what got me through winter. I rejoiced when that last snow melted, and it was time to sing, "Here Comes the Sun."

Today there are times that my spiritual life needs a boost. I get so enmeshed in life's demands that I forget what the sunshine once meant to me. I forget that God's sunny disposition never fades and is always there for me.

For Contemplation
- What long, cold, lonely winters do I experience?
- Who is my sunshine?
- When do I bring sunshine into the lives of those around me?

"Peace I leave with you; my peace I give to you." / John 14:27

It's going to be all right

It seems my peace always comes via the Holy Spirit—and sometimes when I least expect it. One summer evening during a women's miniseries at a monastery, we had time to explore the grounds for a time of personal reflection.

Despite the splendid trees, delightful sunset, and overall quiet, something just wasn't right. Sure, it had been quite a week. But I just felt out of sorts and couldn't pinpoint why. The more I tried to figure it out, the more muddled my feelings became. Soon a very gentle breeze touched my cheek, and I knew it was the Holy Spirit telling me that everything was going to be all right. I didn't get an answer about what was going on, just a feeling that everything would work out.

Imagine my delight when I discovered the following week that I was pregnant with my second child, who now is my beautiful five-year-old daughter.

For Contemplation
- God's peace is there for the taking. Why is it that we often overlook the obvious? What can I do to be more in tune with the peace and harmony God wants for me?
- How can prayer help me move through the foggy, confused moments of life into the peace of Christ?
- How am I open to the gifts that the Holy Spirit has given me to share with others?

My Thoughts

I pray that the God of our Lord Jesus Christ … may give you a spirit of wisdom and revelation as you come to know him, so that, with the eyes of your heart enlightened, you may know what is the hope to which he has called you …. / Ephesians 1:17–18

Marking time

Following are several ways that different families keep track of momentous events—times to be enlightened and hopeful—in their lives:

- Our son and daughter-in-law were so excited when they found out that she was expecting their first child. When they made their initial visit to the doctor, they learned that their baby was two inches long. The first thing our son did when he got home from the doctor's office was to find just the right doorsill and place a mark two inches above the floor. He then dated the mark and continued with this ritual as the baby grew.
- Photo albums are something we have treasured since our dating years. We have chronicled nearly every important moment on film and have attempted to mount them in dated albums, which we frequently peruse. We want the children to enjoy them, yet we really want to protect and preserve the photos. To help contain curious little hands, we have created a special album for each child, filling it with excess photos and their own drawings. This way everyone's happy.
- Happy baptism! In most homes, "Happy Birthday" is a greeting heard each time a family member turns a year older. In our house, we have an additional celebration. We make certain that everyone gets special treatment on the anniversary of his or her baptism. Sometimes we mark the day with a special dinner, a visit to church, or the gift of a treasured book.

For Contemplation
- Do I take time to savor special moments in my life?
- What steps do I take to answer God's call?
- What hopeful ritual would be meaningful to add to my family's routine?

"Righteous Father, the world also does not know you, but I know you, and these know that you sent me. I made your name known to them and I will make it known, so that the love with which you loved me may be in them, and I in them." / John 17:25–26

Get to know me

If you let my foot in the door, you'll love what's in my heart! I can't tell you how many times I've felt this way as we make move after move across the country. Every few years, we pick up and follow a crazy career wherever it takes us. Moving really does rob us of so much time and energy, and then we still have to establish new relationships and routines.

We've moved so frequently that I've learned to accept and trust people. No game playing, no beating around the bush. The problem is that people we meet seem to be wary of us. They're comfortable in their routines, and we're outsiders. We want so much to fit in with our neighbors, wherever we may land. First impressions get tiresome. I worry about the kids fitting in.

The one thing that gives me some sense of security is the wonderful group of friends we have made over the years. They stretch from one end of the country to the other and beyond. Even if we only communicate through yearly Christmas greetings, we know we're there for each other. Our hearts are open. I just wish more strangers felt the same way.

For Contemplation
- What makes me feel lonely?
- Hospitality is so important in developing a sense of community. In what ways does my family extend hospitality to others?
- In my busy life, do I take time to get to know new people? Why or why not?

My Thoughts

It is that very Spirit bearing witness with our spirit that we are children of God …. / Romans 8:16

Get well

The innocent and tender good intentions of my preschoolers are more comforting than any pain medicine I can imagine!

Ouch! One morning my back just snapped as I lifted my fifty-pound son from the floor, where he had been sleeping, to the bed. Later that day he noticed that I was applying heat to my back and asked what I was doing. I explained that I hurt my back. When he asked, "How?" I related the morning's events.

He promptly instructed me not to do *that* again. His brother also noticed my discomfort and inquired about my injury.

The next day each boy, on separate occasions, asked if I was feeling better. I told them I was improving and that in a couple of days, my back would be all better. My five-year-old promptly responded with a handmade get-well card. He gave it to me saying, "I bet now you'll get better *right away*." Later, my four-year-old came to me and said, "Maybe if I kiss it, your back will be *all* better." So I dutifully said, "okay," as I lifted my T-shirt and bent down on my knees. With that, he placed one of those gentle, sweet kisses that only children can give.

In my day-to-day caregiving of the boys, I never imagined there would be times when they would care for me, heal me, and nourish me with their tender love.

For Contemplation
- How do prayers nourish my inner self, bringing strength and vitality?
- Do I take time out when I need some rest, relaxation, and rejuvenation?
- What challenges do I face that sometimes push me to the limit?

My Thoughts

"When he established the heavens, I was there …. / Proverbs 8:27

Knowing heaven

I have often wondered what heaven is like. As a child, I envisioned a pair of feathery-white wings attached to each of our smiling human forms. Heaven was a place where we would frolic all day in the clouds, eating our favorite foods, and doing our favorite things. I cherished this simple view, this pleasant thought. Comfort came from believing that loved ones had passed to this happy place.

Today the heaven in my mind's eye is so much more complex. Perhaps it's the process of getting there in the first place that adds complexity. I cannot envision graceful winged angels with my large thighs. I can no longer fathom angels eating endless German chocolate cakes. I cannot imagine angels hitting the malls for seasonal bargains. My adult vision of heaven is much more ethereal, more spiritual. My brow furrows when I try to figure it out. The promise of this perfect life, this state of total happiness, seems unattainable.

Am I *good* enough to gain entrance through those pearly gates? Will I die in God's grace and friendship? Am I worthy to become one of those spiritual creatures who surround God? Right now, God surrounds me—helping me, guiding me, showing me the path to life eternal. In the grand scheme of things, I suppose it's the getting there that matters, not what it's like once I arrive.

For Contemplation
• What is my image of heaven?
• How am I preparing for life eternal?
• Where do I find my little slice of heaven on earth?

My Thoughts

"This is my body that is for you. Do this in remembrance of me."
    1 Corinthians 11:24

Rituals

I find great comfort in rituals. In eighteen years not a day has
passed that I haven't tucked in my sons, heard their prayers, and
ended the day with, "God bless you. I love you." These few tender
moments bring closure to the day. Sometimes these few minutes
are the only quiet times we have together. This ritual is one
passed on from my mother, one that still plays in my mind as I
crawl into bed each evening.

Going to Mass is another lifelong ritual. The experience was
awe inspiring to a small girl in a huge and ornate East coast
church. The marble floors, huge stained-glass windows, and
imposing altar all glorified God. I remember looking up,
wondering who carved all those arches and statues. For a time the
liturgy was in Latin. While I had no idea what was being said, I
knew it was prayer. I sometimes closed my eyes, drifting to a
comfortable place where I rested with Jesus. I remember being
nudged and told to "Pay attention." Actually, this contemplative
time had more meaning than the mumbo jumbo, but being an
obedient child, I typically got back into the Gospel or Creed or
offertory or whatever.

One part of the Mass I would never miss is the consecration. It
inspired such reverence in a little girl's heart. Still does. Somehow
I see this eucharistic celebration as the ultimate ritual—one that
is the same no matter where or when it is celebrated. It was the
same when I was in Holland as it was when I visited Canada. It
was the same when we moved to Iowa and later to California.
What a wonderful way to remember Christ's ultimate sacrifice.

For Contemplation
+ What is my role in the celebration of the Eucharist?
+ How do I incorporate rituals into my family's life?
+ What activities bring comfort to my soul?

Praise the LORD, all you nations!
  Extol him, all you peoples!
For great is his steadfast love toward us,
  and the faithfulness of the LORD endures forever. / Psalm 117:1–2

Proud godmother

Since the day a dear friend asked me, I have graciously taken on the role of godmother to her daughter, truly an angel of God and a sweet child.

At the age of six, she took on a special role for me. She was the flower girl for my wedding. She came through with such pride and delight. Her incredibly sensitive comments were so touching. When she told me how beautiful I was, it was with deep meaning and sincerity. She even said my husband-to-be was "pretty." I can't even describe my feelings when I saw tears falling from her eyes as she walked down the aisle and reached the altar. She was such a vital part of this sacred union.

I thank God that we are truly involved in each other's lives.

For Contemplation
+ Have I maintained contact with my godparents? Is there anything I can do to strengthen or reestablish this relationship?
+ What role does my child's godparents play in my family life?
+ What do I do to renew my baptismal call?

My Thoughts

"Every kingdom divided against itself becomes a desert ...."
   Luke 11:17

One, two, three ...

As the grandmother of six children who live across the nation, I need to be creative in our relationships. A few years ago, three of my grandchildren visited us in Arizona, prior to being transferred with their parents to Alaska. My three-year-old granddaughter really enjoyed floating in our pool at night while gazing at the stars and moon. We would look into the sky, count to three, and give each other hugs over the moon.

After they left I decided it would be a great idea to connect with her each month. When the moon was full, I would go outside, call her on the phone, and she would go out on her back porch, count to three, and we would give each other a big "hug."

This worked pretty well in Alaska in the wintertime. Summer, however, was a different story! With the days containing up to twenty hours of sunlight, it was almost impossible for a little girl to stay up long enough to see the moon. During one of our July visits to Alaska, we anxiously awaited the arrival of the full moon. Before my granddaughter went to bed, I promised that I would wake her if I saw the moon. Although I couldn't rouse her from a deep sleep, I did pick her up, carry her downstairs, and sit on the porch, holding her while gazing at the moon. The next morning she was very upset that I saw the moon and she didn't.

Once home, a particularly busy month distracted me from the moon phases. One night after I had collapsed in bed, the phone rang. The squealing voice at the other end asked, "Grammy, Grammy, are you ready? I see the moon. Can we count?"

"One, two, three ..."

For Contemplation
* What special rituals have I established with my family?
* How can I make routine activities more meaningful?
* Sometimes holy moments just happen. How can I savor them more fully?

Then he said to her, "Your sins are forgiven ... your faith has saved you; go in peace." / Luke 7:48,50

Be patient

Someone once warned me never to pray for patience. Why? Well, according to my friend, prayers for patience only deliver more trials designed to teach patience the hard way.

Not needing more trials, I really tried to steer clear of specific prayers geared toward patience. Then one day, I saw a quotation by St. Frances de Sales: "Be patient with others," he instructed, "but above all with yourself. I mean do not be disturbed because of your imperfections."

There was the answer to my patience problem. First, I had to try more to understand and tolerate others. So what if the woman in front of me at the grocery store had nothing to do except chat with the store clerk? An extra minute in line wasn't going to greatly alter my day. Clumsy toddlers and messy teens were an ongoing challenge, but somehow God would help me use these challenges as teachable moments.

Next, I had to be patient with myself. So my once-size-eight waist was now a twelve going on fourteen. Getting in shape takes time. After all, it took me a while to get out of shape. My love of clutter wasn't something new. I had been a "collector" since childhood. Some day my house might be orderly. But as long as it is clean, who cares? And, yes, sometimes my concern turns to worry. This imperfection has disturbed me in the past. But, with the advice of St. Frances de Sales, I decided to pray about it rather than fret.

Funny how sometimes a few simple words can help me get back on track.

For Contemplation
- How would I describe my patience level?
- Am I more impatient with myself or others? Why?
- What does it really mean to me to know that God always forgives my shortcomings?

O God, you are my God, I seek you,
  my soul thirsts for you.
    Psalm 63:1

Images of God

It was New Year's weekend, and as usual, the entire family headed out to Mass—my husband and I, our five-year-old son, and three-year-old daughter. What we had forgotten was that due to the holiday, the church nursery was closed, so this week we were all together in "big church." Fortunately, my purse is always stuffed with books, pencils, and paper, which come in handy when trying to help toddlers sit still.

Little did I know that our daughter would challenge both our artistic talents and our concept of God all during the course of Mass.

As our daughter handed a pencil to me, she said, "Mommy, draw a picture of God." My mind went blank as she persisted. All I could come up was a heart to symbolize love. That didn't satisfy her curious mind, so I sat her next to Daddy and whispered her request. He proceeded to draw a picture of Jesus. She wasn't happy with Daddy's image either.

Although we never did draw the right picture for her that morning, I find it fascinating that the search for God has started so intensely at the tender age of three.

For Contemplation
- When did I begin my search for God? What have I discovered?
- What are some of the times that I am most aware of God's thirst-quenching presence?
- What is my image of God?

My Thoughts

"You shall love your neighbor as yourself." / Galatians 5:14

The bus driver and the safety lady

This is a tale of two unlikely public servants who do their jobs not for pay or prestige but as a sort of ministry to their communities' children. There are many thousand such moms (and dads) out there. I, for one, used to take them for granted. Now I pray for these selfless workers daily.

At first I was surprised to hear that a longtime friend had been driving a school bus for several years and planned to continue until her youngest was out of high school. She was far from the physical stereotype of a typical bus driver. Petite, soft-spoken, gentle. She also was an incredibly introspective woman, very involved with her family and her church. Why would she want to get up before daybreak, freeze in the winter, and roast in the summer to drive across dirt roads and through city traffic to deliver children to school? Was she crazy? No, she said, she just wanted to help out and support the small Christian school her children attended.

Then there was "the safety lady," the wife of one of my husband's friends. Her message was one of farm and ranch safety—teaching children to watch out for heavy equipment, to stay clear of danger, and to learn how to handle basic implements. Again, her demeanor seemed incongruous with the task at hand, but she accomplished her mission with joy and enthusiasm.

Both of these women are happy with who they are. They love their neighbors enough to be concerned about their well-being and to give of themselves in service we often take for granted.

For Contemplation
- Before I can truly love my neighbor, I have to love myself. Is there anything that gets in the way?
- Who are the selfless individuals I admire in my community?
- What do I learn when I serve others—in both big and small ways?

"Rejoice that your names are written in heaven." / Luke 10:20

Viewpoints

Sometimes it's downright tough to be positive. There are days when life just doesn't seem to lend itself to optimism. Take Monday. The day started out with a dead battery in the car. It continued with a broken sprinkler spouting water all over our yard and the neighbor's. Then I reached into my purse to grab a pen. What I grabbed was a handful of ink. Somehow, the once-delightful gel pen had become goo that spread all over my wallet and keys and papers. Then the teacher conference was delayed, and my haircut turned out just awful. My son fell on the playground and needed stitches in his chin. Things seemed to deteriorate from there, but I really hate to complain too much.

I feel guilty when I moan about my woes when others have it so much worse than I do. But I'm constantly wondering how to have a more positive outlook when little glitches mar an otherwise great day. I try to be optimistic, I really do. I remind myself of encouraging words and strive to think good thoughts. I share my faults and foibles with my friends. We laugh, we commiserate with one another. But I still sometimes get caught up in a web of frustration with things that go wrong.

Eventually, I remind myself that God is always up there looking out for me, encouraging me, laughing and crying with me. Suddenly things don't seem so overwhelming.

For Contemplation
- What reminders do I have of God's constant love?
- How can I let my family and friends know that I need their encouragement and support?
- Is prayer one of my coping skills? Why or why not?

My Thoughts

"You who seek God, may your hearts be merry!" / Psalm 69:33 (NAB)

Forgiveness

My children have taught me more about forgiveness than I ever imagined. They are so quick to forgive. It comes so naturally to them. They harbor no grudges. I wish I could be more like them.

While I don't harbor huge grudges, I sometimes find it hard to forgive the stupidity of coworkers, friends, and family members. Sure, we all make mistakes. But, when someone is repeatedly insensitive or careless or angry, I find it tough to let go of my frustration with them. It might not be my problem, but I still get caught up in the negative energy rather than modeling myself after my children and saying or thinking, "Okay, I forgive you."

It's incredible that God is like that. All we have to do is ask, and our sins are forgiven. No matter how huge the transgression, God gives us another chance if we just have it in our heart to seek forgiveness.

Because I can't change the behavior of those around me, I've got to change my attitude about their actions. None of us are perfect, so it really isn't fair for me to judge them. Yet sometimes it hurts when hurtful comments make their way back to me or when someone's harsh tone of voice cuts to the quick. God, my sin is not being more forgiving. Help me be more like you.

For Contemplation
• How can I become a more forgiving person?
• Could counseling help me get over some of the long-term grudges I harbor?
• What impact do my emotions have on my physical health?

My Thoughts

Now as they went on their way, he entered a certain village where a woman named Martha welcomed him into her home. ... The Lord answered her, "Martha, Martha, you are worried and distracted by many things ...." / Luke 10:38–41

Perfection

How is it that Marthas everywhere seem to be the perfect hostesses? From the biblical Martha to Martha Stewart, these wonders of humanity have a special knack for making others comfortable. But why is it that I feel so inadequate? As a mom, I'm pretty good at attending to the needs of others—I wipe noses and clean tables, I nurture and guide. I do my best at work and even try to volunteer when I have a chance. But there's always more to be done. Nothing I do seems to be perfect.

When I go to lunch at one friend's house, everything (and I mean everything) is in order. There are no overripe bananas on the windowsill, no empty milk cartons on the counter, no Kleenex scattered around her son's bedroom, no dirty socks dangling from the hamper. How can she do everything right? Have the perfect napkins to match her tablecloth and homemade cookies to boot? My family is lucky to get bakery goods, and that's when they're on sale!

While I know I'm no Susie Homemaker, I really do try to make my home comfortable—a place where people feel welcome, a place where hospitality is important. But I also worry that I just don't measure up to my friends' and family's expectations. It sure would be nice to have a more peaceful feeling around the house.

For Contemplation
- What can I do to bring physical peace and harmony into my home?
- What steps can I take to help enhance spiritual peace and harmony in our home?
- How can I get rid of the nagging guilt and worries that seem to plague me?

"Ask, and it will be given you; search, and you will find; knock, and the door will be opened for you." / Luke 11:9

Already?

Suddenly, all my friends were planning for retirement. Before long I'll be there too. Where, oh where, have the years gone? What will life be like without a set routine? Who ever thought we would make it this far?

Some of us just returned to work fifteen years ago when our children went off to jobs and college. Others are ending brilliant careers as teachers or engineers or nurses.

Of all life's transitions, I feel least prepared for this one. After high school, I knew I was going to college. After college, I knew I was getting married. After marriage, I knew there would be kids. After kids, I knew there would be work. After work, what will there be?

God, I need your help. Thank you for giving me the wake-up call of my friends' retirement. Now I can think and plan and ponder and wonder about my own retirement. What will I do with all my free time? Or will it really be free time? The thought is more exciting than frightening; there are so many options.

Time to garden, perhaps. Time to travel. Time to read. Time to write real letters. Time to visit friends and family. Time to pray, really pray. Maybe I should just sit back and let it happen. Time to learn to trust.

For Contemplation
- What transitions have been smooth in my life? What transitions have been rocky?
- How can I plan for the next phase of my life?
- Who can I turn to for advice and wisdom regarding life's transitions?

My Thoughts

Set your minds on things that are above …. / Colossians 3:2

True faith

In my lifetime, I have encountered only a few very enlightened, truly holy people—those who radiate their deep love of God, their deep understanding of faith, and the joy that comes from focusing on what's important both in this life and the next.

Two of these very holy people recently lost a son to a sudden and unexpected aneurysm. I learned of the death through a friend who called one Sunday afternoon. I felt helpless when I heard about their loss. All I could do was pray.

As I walked into church that evening, I paused when I noticed huge letters, more than a foot tall, spelling out *D-E-A-T-H* on the back wall of the parish hall. The *D* and *E* were filled in with heavy black paint. About halfway through the *A*, that color changed to flowers on a white background. The curious message was explained during church announcements by the youth minister, who said the teens would be having an evening on death. As I left the sanctuary, I thought about our friends' response to death. Certainly they were devastated by the loss but so truly elated by the promise of eternal life that they were able to go on living as God intended. What a blessing to have friends whose words, actions, and thoughts show they are not afraid of moving on to life eternal.

For Contemplation
◆ How do I feel when I contemplate my own death? The death of those I love?
◆ What do I imagine my everlasting dwelling place in heaven will be like?
◆ What does it mean to "Live every day as if it were your last"?

My Thoughts

Now faith is the assurance of things hoped for, the conviction of things not seen. / Hebrews 11:1

My son

On March 23 my life changed forever.

I was so excited about meeting my son for the first time that I barely slept the night before. I felt like a child anticipating Christmas morning. I'm not sure how I got through that Tuesday waiting for the agreed-upon 6:30 P.M. meeting. Somehow I drove myself to the restaurant. When I walked into the restaurant, my eyes went immediately to a tall young man whose back was toward me. He was speaking to the hostess. When he turned, I saw his profile and knew it was him—he looked just like his uncle, my brother. In fact, he looked a lot like me. He was carrying a dozen long-stemmed red roses. I watched as the hostess seated him at his table.

Moments later the hostess returned, took my name, and led me the table where he was seated.

Needless to say, we ate very little that evening as we shared family photographs, histories, and medical information. I answered his inevitable questions of why I had given him up for adoption. We talked about what our lives had been like those past twenty-five years that we were apart. He also asked questions about his father. Before he asked, I told him he should always call me by my name because he only had one mother, the woman who raised him.

In the seven years since that profound, life-changing evening, I have become a mother, publicly, and a grandmother. I am truly blessed to have been given this opportunity to be a part of my son's life and to enjoy life's greatest blessing—grandchildren. It truly has been an honor to meet and get to know the wonderful people who adopted him, his mother and father, and to become a part of their family. We now share birthdays and holidays, including Christmas mornings, with "our" grandchildren. I have been able to express my deep gratitude to them for raising such a wonderful man. Each Mother's Day, I cherish the opportunity to remember his mother, with flowers, a card, and a note of profound appreciation, love, and gratitude.

For Contemplation
+ What have I hoped for deep inside myself? How have I kept that hope alive?
+ How do I react to the unexpected blessings in my life?
+ Where do I find the faith to hold on when situations seem impossible?

My Thoughts

Therefore, since we are surrounded by so great a cloud of witnesses, let us also lay aside every weight and the sin that clings so closely, and let us run with perseverance the race that is set before us, looking to Jesus the pioneer and perfecter of our faith …. / Hebrews 12:1–2

Comfort

Sometimes we can't explain our fears or our pain, but we find comfort in things as close as the infant in our arms or as distant as the moon's shining light. Peace and strength exist amidst the pain.

During the darkest days of my life,
My body shivering in fear,
My heart holding on to hope,
My self being battered by the storm,
I looked up and saw the moon.

While nursing the infant—
Emotions bruised,
My oldest child cried out through the turmoil of our lives,
"Mommy, hold me now! Carry me now!"

Somehow I find the strength to do what God asks,
For, through the light of the moon,
I see that God holds me now, carries me now.

For Contemplation
- What were the darkest days of my life?
- How does giving life and nurturing others give me the strength to go on?
- Who helps me make it through the dark days of life?

My Thoughts

For I know their works and their thoughts, and I am coming to gather all nations and tongues .... / Isaiah 66:18

Twelve were called

As we started a new ministry in our parish, twelve women came forward to serve as leaders. We said yes to a fulfilling but difficult task—that of empowering and nurturing other mothers. We do it so naturally for our children and for our spouses, why not do it for one another?

Well, we came together, this unlikely group of twelve. Our stories were gripping and sometimes frightening. Our lives shared many joys, yet they were colored by abuse, violence, and even death. In spite of challenges, we were empowered by the Spirit with the fire of life. Faith, hope, joy, and love gave each of us the courage to survive. Our ages ranged from the late twenties to early sixties. Among us were two grandmothers, one stepmom, one adoptive mom, and one pregnant mom. Together, we had twenty-seven children and eight grandchildren. During the course of our eight-week journey, one mom lost a grandchild to a fatal disease, another was occasionally debilitated by lupus. Five work outside the home. One is a widow. Two are divorced. Together, we have known the pain of miscarriage and infertility, the rejection of our mothers, the deaths of our mothers, the pain of battery and abuse by alcoholic husbands or fathers. We have known the cross of life and been resurrected to give new life. Each of us had our own story and willingly shared it, that others might learn.

We were the start of something wonderful—not one new ministry but eight—in addition to myriad random acts of kindness.

For Contemplation
- When have I found strength by sharing my life story with others?
- How do I deal with painful experiences from my past?
- How has my life been enriched by listening to others' stories?

My Thoughts

My child, perform your tasks with humility; / then you will be loved by those whom God accepts. / Sirach 3:17

Rescued by prayer and angels

I knew something was wrong when the nurse didn't give my daughter a bag of prenatal goodies as she left the exam room after the first ultrasound. My fears were confirmed a few days later when the second ultrasound revealed that the baby was dead.

A few months later, she was overjoyed to find out she was pregnant again, yet she also feared she would lose this baby too.

Although sick during the first months of pregnancy, by the fifth month, things had calmed down. Then at thirty-four weeks, problems kicked in. Premature labor and preeclampsia were diagnosed. At thirty-seven weeks, we found out she had been leaking amniotic fluid for about two weeks. After she started labor, a fever developed. Complications increased, but our grandson was born. Not only did he have a low Apgar score, but the doctors also told us his mother was "very sick."

After three hours of waiting and hearing nothing new, I made my way into the locked recovery room. What I saw made my knees go weak. My daughter's doctor was holding her legs up to his shoulders. She was completely void of color. Her lips were blue. She was hemorrhaging. They couldn't stop the bleeding.

When the doctors met with us, they told us they didn't expect her to live through the night. I couldn't just sit there. I called anyone I could think of and asked them to start prayer chains. I asked God to send his mighty angels to surround her bed. As she slipped in and out of consciousness, I felt strangely calm. Following a hysterectomy and eventual recovery, this miracle woman looked up at me and said, "Mom, I saw angels."

Our little "angel" is now four years old and the joy of our lives.

For Contemplation
- What miracles have touched my life?
- How does prayer bring me peace?
- What is the greatest gift I can give my family and friends?

So therefore, none of you can become my disciple if you do not give up all your possessions. / Luke 14:33

God's stewardship of gifts given

Although I never really considered myself a worldly person, I do like my creature comforts. Does Christ's command to renounce our worldly possessions mean that I have to give up my monthly manicure? My son's new crib? The computer we finally got after years of saving? This teaching frightens me. I'm not ready to give up my air-conditioning in the summer or my roaring wood-stove in the winter. I don't think I could manage without a car. And I love the antique teacups on the hutch in our dining room. I don't covet these things to the exclusion of living the Gospel—I love my neighbors; heck, I love people I don't even know. I pray all the time. I volunteer at school and church. I try to be a good mom, wife, and daughter. I'm still scared sometimes that I'm not a worthy disciple. But I am following Jesus. I really want to help build my family's foundation in the Lord. We aren't consumed by material things, yet we do enjoy them. They bring us joy but certainly aren't the only joys we share. I treasure my daughter's smile and my husband's hugs. I give thanks for the food on our table. But, Lord, don't ask me to give up that microwave. It's what gets us out the door and to church on time.

For Contemplation
+ How can I balance my desire to follow Christ's teachings and use material things to praise God?
+ How do I practice good stewardship of the spiritual and material gifts I have been given?
+ When is the last time we sat down as a family to discuss our spiritual well-being? Our financial affairs? Our commitment to Christ?

My Thoughts

I received mercy because I had acted ignorantly in unbelief, and the grace of our Lord overflowed for me with the faith and love that are in Christ Jesus. / 1 Timothy 1:13–14

Transformations

I know people can change. I am the perfect example. I was an unhappy mom who felt isolated and found life's little trials to be an excuse to complain rather than a reason to rejoice. Everything seemed like a chore. Dirty diapers to wash. Dishes to do. Tears to wipe. Floors to clean. Errands to run. The list seemed both hopeless and endless. Everything I did seemed to focus on filling someone else's needs. I didn't know when I last read a book. I couldn't take a shower in peace. My friends were so caught up in their own lives that we rarely even talked, let alone got together to share and listen to one another. I was awash in my unhappiness. Drudgery dogged me day and night. I thought this was just the way it was for new mothers.

Then my children went to school, and my isolation ended. I started talking to other mothers, and fathers too. That's all it took. Talking and listening. I learned I wasn't alone. While no one found these chores incredibly exciting, they didn't find them dull and dreadful. I didn't change my attitude overnight, but I did get a new perspective on everyday activities. I began to see these tasks as part of my sacred call, my ministry.

Slowly, I came to experience satisfaction when completing simple tasks. I got organized. I went to the gym. I found play groups that got both mom and tot out more. My eyes were opened to a new way of looking at this vocation of motherhood.

For Contemplation
- Have I ever felt isolated? What did I do with that feeling?
- Where do I go when I need to get a new perspective?
- How could I help someone who needs encouragement?

"Whoever is faithful in a very little is faithful also in much ...."
Luke 16:10

My cheerleader

"Do you have a cheerleader?" I often ask my friends. I'm so sad
when they look at me, puzzled, and say, "A what?"
"A cheerleader," I answer.
Everyone needs a cheerleader. Someone who is there to
support and encourage, praise and prompt. My cheerleader might
wink at me across a crowded church. She calls me just to say it's
raining. She tells me I look wonderful. She creates special
moments even on the most mundane days.
My cheerleader is a woman young enough to be one of my
daughters. She is more than a friend. She is a treasure, a true gem.
She surprises me with flowers on Mother's Day or any day. She
calls me with a joke or an anecdote from her wonderful family.
I can't imagine what life would be like without this spark of
enthusiasm. I really think we all need this kind of friend—
someone who puts our interests before theirs, someone who loves
us just for being us. Someone who helps us when we want to lose
those extra ten pounds, or someone who supports our decision to
be overweight right now. Someone who knows when we need a
hug and who is there to give it. My cheerleader brings so much
incredible joy to my life.

For Contemplation
* Have I ever had a cheerleader? Am I willing to practice being a
  cheerleader for someone?
* When do my eyes sparkle with the radiance of God's love?
* How can the cheerleader image enhance my parenting skills?

My Thoughts

Pursue righteousness, godliness, faith, love, endurance, gentleness.
     1 Timothy 6:11

Just plain fun!

"We had a blast!"

Those four words were a real wake-up call to me one Monday morning. A friend came into work that day describing her family's weekend and announced, "We had a blast!"

While I had been physically awake, I suddenly realized that I had been emotionally asleep for quite some time.

"Had a blast," I thought. "When was the last time I could say that I actually had a blast?"

Sure, parties have been fun. Family trips have been enjoyable. I have a happy life. But "had a blast?" It had been such a long time.

Maybe back when life was free and easy. Before kids and responsibilities and life's complications. Was it in college? High school? That was a long time ago.

So I decided to focus some attention on emotions. What was the difference between having fun and having a blast? What did I need to do to fully enjoy the many blessings and good times in my life? How could I heighten my enthusiasm so that some Monday I could walk into work and announce, "I had a blast"?

While I haven't done it yet, I'm still searching for the right combination.

For Contemplation
+ When was the last time I "had a blast"?
+ How can I "lighten up" and develop my spirit of adventure?
+ What hopes and dreams do I have for my future?

My Thoughts

O LORD, how long shall I cry for help,
and you will not listen? / Habakkuk 1:2

God whispered in my ear

Seven years ago, one of my friends successfully battled breast
cancer—even laughing when she lost her hair. Then, two years
ago, following an illness of several weeks, her doctor encouraged a
return visit to the oncologist. The news was shocking. The cancer
had spread to her liver, spine, and lungs. She faced it all again
with the aid of her husband, family, and friends. She shared the
details so matter-of-factly, yet they were so gruesome. Through it
all, she kept up her routines—swimming, teaching her
third-graders, and riding her horse when she could.

Although we didn't see each other often, we would call or
e-mail when we had a chance. One especially cheerful note
detailed her wonderful weekend at the beach with her husband.
Then the awful news. She was about to begin her seventh bout
with chemo. The radiation hadn't worked. A friend told me the
straight scoop: "She looks awful. Her face is bloated and red.
They can't do radiation for fear of brain damage. We don't know
how much longer she'll be with us."

I was heartbroken. The next day I called her. I swear God was
whispering in my ear. We joked about movies, books, and goofy
jokes. I told her I loved her and that her friendship meant
everything to me. She told me the same. That was the last time I
talked to her. Although I always imagined her dying peacefully in
her sleep, she experienced a painful end following a fall in the
night. I realized then that things happen in God's time and not
ours. God guided this dear friend to her final place of peace. I am
thankful for her gifts of strength and fierce determination.

For Contemplation
- What helps me accept "God's time" when I want things on
  my terms?
- In what instances do I show fierce determination?
- How do I stay in touch with my friends?

O sing to the LORD a new song,
  for he has done marvelous things.
    Psalm 98:1

My Independence Day

My big day had once again arrived. While my children look forward to the Fourth of July in a never-ending quest for the ultimate bottle rocket, I have come to signify July 4 as my personal Independence Day.

For the past few years, I have greeted the sun, donned my Nikes, and headed for the annual July Fourth 5K race. It has become a much-anticipated tradition—those rare twenty-something minutes a year when I can concentrate on just me. This year was a little different, though. With a second-place finish last year, I was striving for nothing less than the first-place trophy this year. It would be my personal gift to myself before turning 4-0 later that summer. Little did I know that the prize I would walk away with would have nothing to do with trophies or engraved letters.

As I headed out the door, my then eleven-year-old son called out, "Can I run with you this year, Mom?"

My heart sank. "Sure, Son," I said, "but I won't be able to wait for you."

There I was, looking into the face of my middle child, who had been diagnosed with epilepsy at age three and had needed so much more care and protection than my other two children. I was telling him that this time he was on his own. This was the little guy who had been so used to being poked with needles that by age four, he seldom flinched when having his blood drawn. And this was the guy whose little body had been slid into a steel cylinder or who had electrodes glued to his scalp on countless occasions—all to pinpoint just what was going wrong in his brain.

About three minutes into the race, with mom and son shoulder to shoulder, I began moving ahead. I glanced back at him. He was keeping his own steady pace. He smiled at me and called out, "Good luck, Mom."

I felt a lump in my throat. He was okay. My son was comfortable going at his own pace. He clearly didn't need his mom by his side. I fought back the tears—tears of joy—as the distance between me and my son grew wider and wider.

That day I finished with my best personal time. Yet the trophy I took home that day means nothing compared to the prize that will stay engraved on this mother's heart forever.

For Contemplation
- What does this story touch in my heart? How do I describe the memorable victories in my life?
- What are some of the lessons I learn from my children and/or grandchildren?
- Do I take time to do things that give me energy and fuel my soul? Why or why not?

My Thoughts

Then Jesus told them a parable about their need to pray always and not to lose heart. / Luke 18:1

My prayer

Dear Lord,

Thank you for blessing me with my little boy. He was such a surprise to us at birth. Two-and-a-half years later, he continues to surprise us. His tender surprises often come when we least expect them.

I'm always rushed to get breakfast on the table, brew the morning coffee, and get out his vitamins. One ordinary morning as he was sitting in his chair, I just plopped down with my coffee and was ready to sink my teeth into a spoonful of Raisin Bran, when I heard him remind me, "Mom, we have to say grace."

He reached his hand toward mine. I put down my spoon and took his small hand as he proudly recited, "Thank you for the world so sweet. Thank you for the food we eat. Amen."

Not only did I now know it was okay to start eating breakfast, but I knew it was an excellent way to start the day.

Thank you, Lord, for these gentle and tender surprises.

For Contemplation
- What tender lessons have I learned from my children?
- What is the biggest surprise I have ever experienced? What made it so special?
- How do I relish sacred moments of God's grace in my life?

My Thoughts

For he is a God of justice,
  who knows no favorites.
Though not unduly partial toward the weak,
  yet he hears the cry of the oppressed.
      Sirach 35:12 (NAB)

Nana's favorite birthday gift

The occasion was the celebration of my grandmother's sixtieth birthday. When we decided to throw a surprise party for this very special person, we knew the guest list would be quite long. Part of the surprise was that our family would make the eighteen-hour drive to be there for the festivities. Well, the surprise was tremendous. Nana was so filled with happiness that she literally sobbed for the first fifteen minutes after her arrival. She has a very special relationship with our sons, ages four and five. Not surprisingly, she was overwhelmed to find them there, along with eighty other friends and family members.

With no prompting at all, our five-year-old (who loves being the center of attention and couldn't resist the captive audience) stood up and started telling the story of Jesus feeding a huge crowd of people with just a few loaves and fishes. He told the story so eloquently that he silenced everyone in the room. He was in his element, especially with the clapping and cheering at the end of the story. Then the little showman invited everyone to join in singing a very heartfelt rendition of "God Bless America." To this day, my grandmother relishes recounting the story of her favorite sixtieth birthday gift.

For Contemplation
- What do I do to make family gatherings joy-filled times?
- How do I reduce the stress sometimes associated with family gatherings?
- How do I nurture my children's relationships with older people?

My Thoughts

The LORD is gracious and merciful,
  slow to anger and abounding in steadfast love.
The LORD is good to all,
  and his compassion is over all that he has made. / Psalm 145:8–9

Prayers answered

I met my husband, who is a quadriplegic, eight years after his accident. When we married, we knew that most likely we would not be able to have our own children—although we did try. It was also difficult to be accepted by a state or private adoption agency due to his disability. However, after four years of prayer and persistence, we were accepted. We revealed our entire financial, emotional, and factual stories and were placed on a Catholic Social Services waiting list.

After two more years of praying, waiting, longing, and listening, the long-awaited phone call came. "You have a baby boy. Can you come and pick him up tomorrow?"

The joy of that moment cannot be described. We were part of a base community group who came to our rescue with all forms of help—from laundry to casseroles. The next day we received our pastor's blessing and drove one hundred miles to pick up our new son, whom we named for the beloved pastor who supported and inspired us. Seeing those baby brown eyes, hearing that angelic cry as the caseworker placed him in my arms were the most grace-filled moments in my life. I didn't give him life—for that we are thankful to his birth mother—but I was ready to love and care for this great joy in our lives. That was seventeen years ago, and he is still a great joy in my life.

For Contemplation
- Large and small grace-filled moments are part of our lives. How have these moments inspired and changed me?
- How do I mark the passing years for my children or grandchildren?
- What are some faith-filled stories that I pass on to others?

Now may our Lord Jesus Christ himself and God our Father, who loved us and through grace gave us eternal comfort and good hope, comfort your hearts and strengthen them in every good work and word.
    2 Thessalonians 2:16

Coming of age

An impromptu ritual we created for my daughter when she came of age was a grace-filled opportunity to pass on wisdom and symbolic gifts. Here are some of the words I wrote for her:

On the day you were born, I never thought you would grow up and move away from me. My heart still responds to your cry, your pain, your joy. Once connected in the womb by the cord of life, we shall always be connected. No one, not even us, can break that bond.

To be a woman is difficult.
To be a woman is divine.
To be a woman can feel like a treacherous uphill climb.
To be a woman can feel fine, flowing loving understanding only as
    a woman can ...

... As you step from girlhood to womanhood, I ask this blessing for you: May you continue to unfold the petals of the flower, the self within you, to allow it to bloom and shine from deep within you; to touch the world in your own special way, but to stay connected at your roots to the earth; to be grounded as you seek, as you spread your wings to fly. I love you.

For Contemplation
+ How do I celebrate my womanhood?
+ What rituals bring comfort when there are changes in my life or that of my family?
+ When someone near and dear to me is ready to spread his or her wings, how can I encourage and empower that person?

"I will give you words and a wisdom that none of your opponents will be able to withstand or contradict." / Luke 21:15

Tag, you're it!

"Tag, you're it," I said as I hung up the phone from yet another returned phone call. Our attempts to communicate—not some cute childhood game—were at issue here. Somehow, it seems that so many of my relationships are turning from personal encounters to a series of brief messages and chance meetings.

For all the conveniences life brings, it also delivers complications. We call for simple dentist or doctor appointments and have to wait weeks—unless the problem is an emergency. Then, if there is a real crisis, we wait for hours in a beeping, buzzing emergency room. When our cars need repair, we no longer drive right up to a friendly service advisor. At big dealerships, the procedure is to call ahead, to be put on hold, then schedule an appointment, eventually show up, wait in line for a while—you get the picture. It's understandable that large offices need efficient receptionists to help control both walk-in and phone-in traffic, but some of these folks tend to be gatekeepers who make it tough for us to get in touch with teachers or brokers or agents or salespeople. We leave yet another message and wait for a return call.

I try to remember that people, real people, are on the other side of every desk and at the other end of every phone line. But, sometimes, it seems all we do is play "tag."

For Contemplation
- What do I do when the complications of daily life get burdensome?
- How can I bring Christ into even the simplest of encounters with others?
- In what ways can technology uncomplicate my life?

My Thoughts

… for in him all things in heaven and on earth were created, things visible and invisible …. / Colossians 1:16

A real job

My daughter was nine months old; my oldest son, four-and-a-half years old. I had decided to finally use my college degree and begin working full time as a registered nurse. I chased job opportunity after job opportunity. I diligently arranged loving child care and eagerly looked forward to a career outside my home. My husband, who preferred me to be a full-time mom, supported my endeavor. From the beginning, he encouraged me to find true meaning and satisfaction in raising our children.

I was determined to find a real job with real life opportunities. My female role models had always worked. My mother kept inquiring when I was going to do something for myself and go to work. (She still does.)

Just as my resumes were mailed out and job interviews began, something quite unexpected happened. I was weak, tired. When I confirmed my pregnancy, I was shocked. My daughter was still a baby, and my career plans were again on hold.

Well, four years have passed, and my nursing career is still on hold, but my whole outlook has changed. God has promised to bless me for my patience and my commitment to my three children. I realize that the perfect job waits for me when I am ready, in my time and not dictated by people who live outside my home. Nursing can wait; my children can't.

For Contemplation
- There is no single work arrangement that fits all mothers. Am I comfortable with the family-work balance I have chosen?
- When do I allow myself to be swayed by outside influences?
- Do I clearly see the blessings God places in my grasp?

My Thoughts

APPENDIX: MOMSharing —
Using MOMStories in Group Settings

Background: MOMStories and MOMS

For those who have been part of the Ministry of Mothers Sharing (MOMS), it's no secret that the ministry's success is largely attributable to you and your willingness to share your spirit-filled stories as mothers.

Although the history of MOMS goes back only a decade, the energy that fuels it is as old as time itself. God gave us the wonderful gift of life in our vocation of motherhood. It is through God's grace that we continue to become more aware of the sacredness of our call to motherhood and to the challenges of personal growth. It is these challenges that prompted Sister Paula Hagen, then a coordinator of family ministry, to work with mothers in the parish to develop a ministry designed to provide support, companionship, and a spiritual boost for women who share one role in common: motherhood. Sister Paula taught mothers to create a safe, sacred, and welcoming environment in which they could nourish their souls and share their stories. The ministry has welcomed many mothers back to their place of worship. It has opened the doors to many other ministries.

As this parish-based ministry expanded, requests for materials and support started pouring in from neighboring churches and, soon, from across the country. That's when Sister Paula and I joined our creative talents to write MOMS: A Personal Journal, summarizing key elements of journal writing, sharing stories, and prayer rituals. From there, Patricia Hoyt helped structure the ministry with materials designed for MOMS facilitators and staff developers. Today, the impact of the ministry is seen everywhere from Alaska to Florida, thanks to the dedication of women of all ages across the nation. With the addition of a video (MOMS: What Is It?), leaders are able to provide interested groups with rapid access to an introduction to the spirit-filled ministry.

MOMStories is an opportunity for us to continue sharing the enthusiasm we experience in our MOMS groups, retreats, and celebrations. For those who want to use MOMStories for ongoing groups, the ministry's founder, Sister Paula Hagen, has developed a format for ongoing groups, which appears on the next pages.

Suggested Format for Using MOMStories to Continue the Journey

For those who have participated in the eight-week MOMS program, the three-member Facilitator Team is one way to simplify the preparation process for using MOMStories in your follow-up group. Members of your group can share the responsibility for these tasks by individually reading Scripture for the upcoming Sunday from their Bibles or from *At Home with the Word* and the appropriate MOMStory for that Sunday (see pages 70–72 for Index of Weekly Scripture Readings: Cycle C).

- **Presenter:** Assign Scripture reading ahead of your session so that everyone comes prepared to share her thoughts. Set up expectations that each participant come having already read the materials and answered the questions that accompany the week's MOMStory.

- **Facilitator Team:** Gather fifteen minutes before the scheduled starting time for last-minute room preparations, name tags, music, etc. Be sure you start and end on time.

- **Prayer Leader:** Light the Christ candle. Have a few minutes of silence and lead the group in saying a gathering prayer.

- **Guardian Angel:** Invite each woman to share any "grace-filled" event, situation, or insight since the last meeting.

- **Presenter:** Have participants read the Scripture for the Sunday to be discussed and invite anyone in the group to share her thoughts on what the passage meant in her life.

- **Guardian Angel:** Read from MOMStories for the same Sunday, inviting the sharing process to continue.

- **Presenter:** Read the discussion questions one at a time. Go around the group, inviting each person to share her answers.

- **Guardian Angel:** Alert the group when there are only ten minutes left in the session.

- **Prayer Leader:** Play quiet music to set a meditative or reflective tone, inviting each woman to pray for the grace to integrate Scripture and Christ's life into her own "mom story."

- **Guardian Angel:** Remind the entire group of the time and place where you will meet and of the assigned readings.

- **Facilitator Team:** If everyone has not received a copy of the "Group Rules for Ongoing Groups" (on the next page), make certain each person receives a copy. Be sure the leaders model the Group Rules in their behavior. When participants do not follow these rules, the group can easily lose its focus.

For copies of At Home With The Word call (800) 933-1800 or fax (800) 933-7094.

Rules for Ongoing Groups

- **Punctuality:** Start and end on time. I will be punctual.

- **Anonymity:** I will not reveal what someone else has personally shared in the group with anyone outside the group.

- **Respect and Trust:** I will respect the right of each person to have her own thoughts, feelings, and beliefs based on her knowledge and life experience. I will trust that my dignity and life experience will be respected as well.

- **Non-Judgment:** I will not judge others. Feelings are not right or wrong. Each person has unique, valuable life experiences.

- **Gentleness:** I will be kind and gentle with myself and others. Hurting persons tend to reach out and hurt other persons. Healing persons tend to reach out with healing compassion.

- **Listening:** I will listen attentively and will not interrupt when another person is talking.

- **Sharing:** I will focus on my true self and try to use first person (I, me, myself) in my conversation. I give myself the freedom to share or pass. I will allow time for each person to share.

- **Rescuing:** I will not preach, editorialize, give advice, or try to problem-solve and/or rescue others. Each person has an ability to solve her own problems.

- **Cross-Talk and Interruptions:** I will not laugh at someone who is talking. I will not talk to others during another person's sharing. I will not interrupt.

- **Mutual Responsibility:** As the group continues to meet, I will take my turn as facilitator. Leadership rotates among the members; this allows me to strengthen my facilitator/leadership skills at my own pace.

Index

Index of Weekly Scripture Readings: Cycle C

Sunday	First Reading	Psalm	Second Reading	Gospel	Page
Palm Sunday	Isa 50:4–7	Ps 22:8–9,17–18, 19–20,23–24	Phil 2:6–11	Lk 22:14–23:56 or 23:1–49	24
Easter	Acts 10:34a,37–43	Ps 118:1–2,16–17, 22–23	Col 3:1–4 or 1 Cor 5:6b–8	John 20:1–9	25
2nd Easter	Acts 5:12–16	Ps 118:2–4,13–15, 22–24	Rev 1:9–11a,12–13,17–19	John 20:19–31	26
3rd Easter	Acts 5:27–32, 40b–41	Ps 30:2–4,5–6, 11–12a,13b	Rev 5:11–14	John 21:1–19 or 21:1–14	27
4th Easter	Acts 13:14,43–52	Ps 100:1–2,3,5	Rev 7:9,14b–17	John 10:27–30	28
5th Easter	Acts 14:21–27	Ps 145:8–9,10–11, 12–13	Rev 21:1–5a	John 13:31–33a, 34–35	29
6th Easter	Acts 15:1–2,22–29	Ps 67:2–3,5,6,8	Rev 21:10–14,22–23	John 14:23–29	30
Ascension	Acts 1:1–11	Ps 47:2–3,6–7,8–9	Eph 1:17–23 or Eph 4:1–13 or 4:1–7,11–13	Luke 24:46–53	31
7th Sunday	Acts 7:55–60	Ps 97:1–2,6–7,9	Rev 22:12–14,16–17,20	John 17:20–26	32
Pentecost	Acts 2:1–11	Ps 104:1,24,29–30, 31,34	1 Cor 12:3b–7,12–13 or Rom 8:8–17	John 20:19–23 or John 14:14–16, 23b–26	33
Holy Trinity	Prv 8:22–31	Ps 33:4–5,6,9,18–19, 20,22	Rom 5:1–5	John 16:12–15	34
Body and Blood of Jesus	Gn 14:18–20	Ps 110:1,2,3,4	1 Cor 11:23–26	Luke 9:11b–17	35
9th Ordinary	1 Kgs 8:41–43	Ps 117:1–2	Gal 1:1–2,6–10	Luke 7:1–10	36
10th Ordinary	1 Kgs 17:17–24	Ps 30:2,4,5–6, 11–12a,13b	Gal 1:11–19	Luke 7:11–17	37
11th Ordinary	2 Sam 12:7–10,13	Ps 32:1–2,5,7,11	Gal 2:16,19–21	Luke 7:36—8:3 or 7:36–50	38
12th Ordinary	Zech 12:10–11; 13:1	Ps 63:2,3–4,5–6,8–9	Gal 3:26–29	Luke 9:18–24	39
13th Ordinary	1 Kgs 19:16b,19–21	Ps 16:1–2a,5,7–8, 9–10,11	Gal 5:1,13–18	Luke 9:51–62	40
14th Ordinary	Isa 66:10–14c	Ps 66:1–3,4–5,6–7, 16,20	Gal 6:14–18	Luke 10:1–12, 17–20 or 10:1–9	41
15th Ordinary	Deut 30:10–14	Ps 69:14,17,30–31, 33–34,36,37	Col 1:15–20	Luke 10:25–37	42
16th Ordinary	Gen 18:1–10a	Ps 15:2–5	Col 1:24–28	Luke 10:38–42	43
17th Ordinary	Gen 18:20–32	Ps 138:1–3, 6–8	Col 2:12–14	Luke 11:1–13	44
18th Ordinary	Eccl 1:2,2:21–23	Ps 90:3–6,12–14,17	Col 3:1–5,9–11	Luke 12:13–21	45
19th Ordinary	Wis 18:6–9	Ps 33:1,12,18–19, 20–22	Heb 11:1–2,8–19 or 11:1–2,8–12	Luke 12:32–48 or 12:35–40	46–47
20th Ordinary	Jer 38:4–6,8–10	Ps 40:2,3,4,18	Heb 12:1–4	Luke 12:49–53	48
21st Ordinary	Isa 66:18–21	Ps 117:1,2	Heb 12:5–7,11–13	Luke 13:22–30	49

Sunday	First Reading	Psalm	Second Reading	Gospel	Page
22nd Ordinary	Sir 3:17–18,20, 28–29	Ps 68:4–5,6–7,10–11	Heb 12:18–19,22–24a	Luke 14:1,7–14	50
23rd Ordinary	Wis 9:13–18b	Ps 90:3–4,5–6,12–13, 14–17	Phlm 9–10,12–17	Luke 14:25–33	51
24th Ordinary	Exod 32:7–11, 13–14	Ps 51:3–4,12–13, 17,19	1 Tim 1:12–17	Luke 15:1–32 or 15:1–10	52
25th Ordinary	Amos 8:4–7	Ps 113:1–2,4–6,7–8	1 Tim 2:1–8	Luke 16:1–13 or 16:10–13	53
26th Ordinary	Amos 6:1a,4–7	Ps 146:7–10	1 Tim 6:11–16	Luke 16:19–31	54
27th Ordinary	Habb 1:2–3,2:2–4	Ps 95:1–2,6–7,8–9	2 Tim 1:6–8,13–14	Luke 17:5–10	55
28th Ordinary	2 Kgs 5:14–17	Ps 98:1–4	2 Tim 2:8–13	Luke 17:11–19	56–57
29th Ordinary	Exod 17:8–13	Ps 121:1–8	2 Tim 3:14—4:2	Luke 18:1–8	58
30th Ordinary	Sir 35:12–14,16–18	Ps 34:2–3,17–18, 19,23	2 Tim 4:6–8,16–18	Luke 18:9–14	59
31st Ordinary	Wis 11:22–12:2	Ps 145:1–2,8–9, 10–11,13b–14	2 Thess 1:11—2:2	Luke 19:1–10	60
32nd Ordinary	2 Macc 7:1–2,9–14	Ps 17:1,5–6,8,15	2 Thess 2:16—3:5	Luke 20:27–38 or 20:27,34–38	61
33rd Ordinary	Mal 3:19–20a	Ps 98:5–6,7–8,9	2 Thess 3:7–12	Luke 21:5–19	62
Christ the King	2 Sam 5:1–3	Ps 122:1–5	Col 1:12–20	Luke 23:35–43	63